Needing
a Friend

Story by Dawn McMillan

Illustrations by Meredith Thomas

Rigby PM Plus Chapter Books
part of the Rigby PM Program
Ruby Level

U.S. edition © 2003 Rigby Education
Harcourt Achieve Inc.
10801 N. MoPac Expressway
Building #3
Austin, TX 78759
www.harcourtachieve.com

Text © 2003 Thomson Learning Australia
Illustrations © 2003 Thomson Learning Australia
Originally published in Australia by Thomson Learning Australia

10 9 8 7 6 5 4
09

Needing a Friend
   ISBN 0 75786 895 9

Printed in China by 1010 Printing International Ltd.

Contents

Chapter 1

Someone New

On the first morning after spring break, Tony waited at the school gates for Jeff to arrive. The bus was late. He looked down the road again, and at last he could see it coming. As it pulled into the stop, Tony saw Jeff at the window and waved. The students stepped off the bus, calling excitedly to their friends.

"Hey, Tony!" shouted Jeff. "Great to see you!"

"You too!" Tony replied. He gave Jeff a friendly push, and they laughed together.

The bell rang and they all rushed in to put their bags away and head into class. Mrs. Hogart was there, smiling and chatting to everyone. The chatter stopped as she walked to the front of the room.

"Good morning, everybody," she said. "This morning we have a new student joining our class," she smiled. "His name is Jamie. Jamie's mom has asked me to talk to you before he arrives. She thinks it's a good idea for you to know a little about him."

Tony looked at Jeff. "I wonder what's so special about him?" he whispered.

Mrs. Hogart continued. "Jamie has Asperger Syndrome," she said. "Does anyone here know anything about Asperger Syndrome?"

Everyone was silent.

"Asperger Syndrome is a condition that can make people behave in different ways from most other people," said Mrs. Hogart. "Often they have problems making friends, and sometimes they seem to be in a world of their own."

Jeff raised his hand. "How did Jamie get Asperger Syndrome?" he asked.

"Good question, Jeff," answered Mrs. Hogart. "Jamie was born with the condition. He is a very intelligent person. People who have Asperger Syndrome are often very interested in one special thing and become experts in that subject. Jamie is very good at math, and he knows all about animals."

Mrs. Hogart continued. "Jamie may not want to join in with all of your talking. Sometimes he doesn't understand jokes so he might feel left out if you are having fun, and he doesn't like it if anyone comes too close to him."

"How can we help him to feel at home?" asked Jeff.

"First of all, we need to keep to our schedule and classroom rules," answered Mrs. Hogart. "Jamie doesn't like too many changes or surprises. He may get upset if he becomes confused. We need to accept that he may do things in a different way."

"Jamie might teach us better ways of doing our work!" laughed Tony.

Mrs. Hogart laughed too. "That's a good thought!" she said. "We're always looking for new ideas. And it won't do us any harm to stick to our routines and rules either!" she grinned. "We might get a lot more done!"

Chapter 2

Math Magic

Jamie stood at the door with his mom and the principal. His head was down and his hair fell across his cheek.

"Hello, Jamie," Mrs. Hogart smiled, as she showed him to his desk.

When his mom and the principal left, Jamie took his pens from his pencil case and lined them up neatly in a row. Then he took his ruler and placed it under the pens.

Tony leaned forward in his desk. "Hi, Jamie," he said.

Jamie looked at Tony and put his head down again.

"We'll start with our math lesson," said Mrs. Hogart. "Today we're going to explore the different ways we can solve a problem. You can work in teams, and you'll need to be able to tell the class how you found the solution."

Tony and Jeff went over to Jamie. "Like to join us?" Jeff asked. Jamie stood up, collected his pens and ruler, and followed the boys to the front of the room.

"Right!" said Tony, looking at the problem written on the board. "What are we going to do to find the answer to this one?"

Jamie looked at the board, then at the boys. "It's 1,220," he said.

"How do you know?" asked Jeff. "How did you work it out so quickly?"

Jamie was quiet. "I just know!" he said.

Jeff and Tony looked at each other and shrugged. Their team had the answer but who was going to explain how they got it?

$$3^4 + 4^3 + 9^3 + 26 + (9^2 \times 2^2) - 4 = ?$$

Chapter 3

Jamie Meets Susie

Later that week, Tony and Jeff asked Jamie to join them in shooting some baskets after school. At first Jamie stood at the edge of the court and watched. Then he moved in to take the ball. He shot basket after basket.

"Hey! How about a turn for us?" Jeff called.

Tony raced in and got the ball. He threw it to Jeff, and then Jamie lost interest and walked away.

Tony shook his head and muttered, "It's going to be tough trying to understand someone like Jamie."

When Tony got home from school, he raced through the side gate to the back of the house.

"Hello, Susie!" he called. "I'm home!"

A small black, brown, and white dog burst out of the back door and jumped up on Tony, barking with excitement.

"Hold on, girl," Tony laughed. "Just let me get something to drink, and then we'll go for our run in the park!"

Tony clipped a leash to Susie's collar, and they set off across the road to the park. Susie barked and pulled at the leash.

"Okay," grinned Tony. "Here we go! Not too fast now, girl. I'm training for basketball not for sprinting!"

With one more bark from Susie they were off, around the edge of the park and through the trees near the skateboard ramp, then around the park again.

"Stop, Susie!" puffed Tony. "I need a rest!"

Tony sat on the bench near the trees. Then he saw Jamie sitting quietly by the ramp, with his skateboard at his feet, and he and Susie walked over to him.

Jamie reached out and patted Susie. "She's a Smooth Fox Terrier," he said. "They used to be called English Terriers and were bred to be working dogs. They're quick enough to catch rats, mice, and rabbits."

Tony was amazed.

Jamie kept his eyes on the dog. "They make good pets because they are very intelligent and friendly, and they're easy to keep clean."

"Wow!" exclaimed Tony. "You know a lot about dogs, as well as being great at math!" he laughed. Tony paused. "Her name's Susie," he said.

Jamie patted the dog again. "Susie," he said quietly. "Susie!" he repeated, more loudly this time.

"She likes you!" laughed Tony.

Tony and Jamie and Susie walked across the park, back to the road.

"Come over to my house, Jamie," said Tony. "You can have some more time with Susie, and we can play basketball."

Jamie seemed not to hear Tony's invitation. They crossed the road, and he turned and walked in the opposite direction.

Chapter 4

Off the Leash

The next afternoon when Tony took Susie to the park, Jamie was waiting for them.

"Hi, Jamie!" Tony called as he ran onto the grass. "Susie's pleased to see you again." He laughed as the little dog pulled against the leash. Jamie knelt down and ran his hand down the dog's back.

"She's still growing," Jamie said.

"Oh," said Tony. "I thought she wouldn't get much bigger!"

Susie rolled over onto her back, and Jamie rubbed her under the chin.

Tony chuckled. "Looks like I'm running on my own today!"

"That's it for the day," puffed Tony as he finished his run. He fastened Susie's leash to her collar, and they all walked toward the road.

"Would you like to come home with us, Jamie? Jeff's coming over later," he said.

Jamie was quiet.

"We can call your mom," offered Tony. "So she knows where you are."

Suddenly Tony felt the leash swing loose in his hand. Then he heard the squeal of brakes. "Susie!" he screamed.

For Tony everything seemed to move in slow motion. A red car pulled to the side of the road. Jamie was there by the dog's side. Everybody was talking at once.

"I'm sorry!" cried the driver. "The dog ran straight in front of me!"

"Don't pick her up!" shouted Jamie. "I'll roll her onto my vest and we'll lift her off the road."

Tony heard his own voice. "The leash came undone!"

They all huddled around Susie on the pavement. Jamie was running his hands over her. "I think her hip is broken," he said. "The spine seems OK."

Susie opened her eyes and tried to struggle to her feet, yelping with pain.

Tony fought back his tears. "What should we do?" he asked in a whisper.

Jamie put his hand on Susie's head. "Quiet now," he said. "We'll take you home." He scooped the dog into his arms with one hand supporting the broken hip, and followed Tony home.

Chapter 5

A Painful Injury

"Dad!" screamed Tony as he raced up the drive. "Susie's been hit by a car! We think she's got a broken hip! Jamie's got her."

Susie was lying quietly in Jamie's arms as they came toward the house.

"We'll take her to the vet," said Dad. "Can you get her into the car, Jamie?"

Dad held the back door open, and Jamie slid in gently. Susie lifted her head and yelped. "Quiet now," whispered Jamie again.

"You've sure got a way with animals, Jamie," said Dad.

At the office, the vet looked at Susie. "The hip's broken all right," she said. "I can't understand why she's so calm. Such a painful injury!"

"It's Jamie," Tony said. "He's been talking to her."

"Well, don't worry too much about Susie. We'll give her something for the pain. We'll have to operate and pin her hip. She'll need looking after for a while, but she'll heal," the vet reassured them.

Out at the car, Tony turned to Jamie.

"Thanks, Jamie!" he said. "Susie and I couldn't have managed without you!"

A shy smile crossed Jamie's face.

"Come on, Jamie," said Dad. "Let's get you home. Your mom will be wondering what's happened to you."

The next day, after school, Jamie went with Tony and Jeff to see Susie. The three of them stood by the large cage where Susie lay.

"It looks like she's in a real hospital," whispered Jeff. "Look at the tubes in her!"

"Poor Susie," Tony said. "You'll be better soon, girl."

Jamie knelt quietly near Susie's head.

"What's going to happen to Susie when we go away to boarding school?" Jeff asked Tony.

Jamie stood up and stiffened. He stared at Tony, then turned and bumped into the doorway as he ran out of the room.

"What's wrong with him?" asked Jeff.

Tony frowned. "I guess he didn't know that I was going away. We're friends now, you know. Although I think he likes Susie even more than he likes me!"

"Well, what *is* going to happen to Susie?" asked Jeff again.

"Mom and Dad say they'll look after her," replied Tony.

Susie whimpered.

"Let's not talk about it any more," whispered Tony. "I think she knows what we are saying."

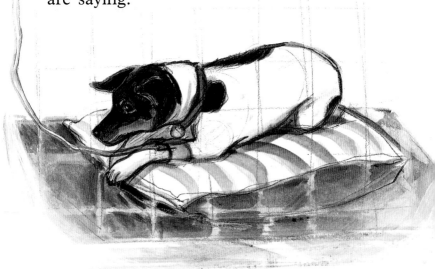

Chapter 6

Taking Care of Susie

Later that night, as Tony lay in bed, he buried his head in the pillow. Until now, going away to boarding school had seemed far away in the future. Tonight he thought about it being next fall. Only a summer away! How could he be apart from Susie? He fell into a light sleep and dreamed of Susie limping around the park, trailing her leash behind her.

The next morning, Tony woke up feeling unhappy. He ate his breakfast in silence.

"Don't worry about Susie," said Dad quietly. "She's fit and strong, and she's young. She'll recover quickly. The vet said she was very pleased with the way the surgery went."

"She might limp!" snapped Tony. "I don't want Susie to have a limp! And what about next fall? What's going to happen to Susie when I go away?"

Mom came into the kitchen. "We'll look after her, Tony," she said. "We'll do the best we can."

Tony stood up from the table. "I know that, Mom," he said softly, "but you haven't got much time, and Susie will need special care now."

"We'll work something out, Tony," Dad said. "We'll talk about it again tonight."

When Tony arrived at the school gate, his friends were already heading into class. He scuffed his feet as he went up the sidewalk toward the classroom.

Jeff turned around and saw him. "Hi, Tony. Any more news of Susie?" he called.

Tony shook his head.

"Hey! She'll be all right," Jeff reassured him.

Tony nodded. Then he saw Jamie standing against the outside wall of the building. "Hi, Jamie!" he called.

Jamie put his head down and walked away.

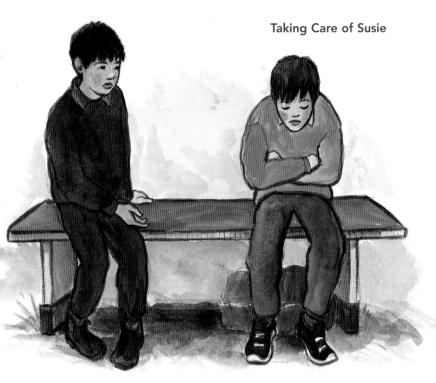

Suddenly Tony knew what to do for Susie! He would ask Jamie to help care for her. He put his bag down, and went over to join Jamie on the bench where he was sitting, taking care not to sit too close.

"Jamie," he said quietly, "I'm sorry I have to go away next fall, but Susie isn't going anywhere. She needs a friend, Jamie, and she really likes you. Will you help Mom and Dad look after her? Take her for walks? Talk to her? Please!"

Jamie turned to Tony. He nodded his head. "I'll look after Susie," he said.

Tony beamed. Without thinking, he slid along the bench next to Jamie. He put his hand on his shoulder and said, "Thanks Jamie!"

Jamie lifted his eyes and looked at Tony. "You're a special friend, Tony," he said, "and Susie's a special friend too." He grinned and stood up. "Two friends!" he said, and he and Tony walked to class together.